Praise for *Blessings for the Long Night: Poems and Meditations to Help You through Depression*

"With *Blessings for the Long Night*, Jessica Kantrowitz is not just a poet, but a tender witness who knows the dark, and a steady companion who will stay until dawn."

—Glennon Doyle, author of the #1 *New York Times* Bestseller *Untamed*, and Founder of Together Rising

"In our most recent and peculiar season, where each of us is unmoored, pressing through, or weighed down, these words anoint and sustain. Jessica Kantrowitz's intimate knowledge of the terrain and her steady presence, both on social media and here in these pages, welcome and bless a weary soul."

—Deidra Riggs, author of *ONE: Unity in a Divided World*; Justice, Equity, Diversity, and Inclusion (JEDI) coach

"This book is a wonderful prayer, words for those who need to know they are not alone in this world. Jessica Kantrowitz offers us grace and companionship through gentle pages that encourage readers to trust, feel, and thrive."

—Tanaya Winder, author of *Why Storms Are Named after People and Bullets Remain Nameless*, musician, and motivational speaker

"Depression may not be your particular 'noonday demon,' but it is for someone you love. And there's no better guide to that interior landscape than Jessica Kantrowitz. For the sufferer, this entire book is a warm blanket, a gentle hug, a wounded healer bringing hot tea and your favorite snack. 'Peace,' says the healer. 'Rest. We will wait with you.'"

—Sarah Arthur, author of *A Light So Lovely: The Spiritual Legacy of Madeleine L'Engle*

"In the midst of the darkness of these times, Jessica's words in *Blessings for the Long Night* are a bright beacon of light to those who are doing their best to keep on keeping on."

—Rev. Nick F. Scutari, Pastor, First UMC New Ulm, Minnesota

"So many people in these hard days are telling us to take deep breaths. But when Jessica Kantrowitz says it—when her poems say it—your body actually obeys. When Jessica's poems say 'anoint,' 'bless,' 'ordain'—you get taller. Your eyes open wider. You step forth. To read this book is to connect your depleted soul to a current of understanding and patience and strength that will light not only your darkness, but others' as well."

—Judith Kunst, author of *The Burning Word and The Way Through*

BLESSINGS FOR THE
LONG NIGHT

BLESSINGS
FOR THE
LONG
NIGHT

Poems and Meditations
to Help You through
Depression

JESSICA KANTROWITZ

BROADLEAF BOOKS
MINNEAPOLIS

BLESSINGS FOR THE LONG NIGHT
Poems and Meditations to Help You through Depression

Cover design: Lindsey Owens

Print ISBN: 978-1-5064-8039-8
eBook ISBN: 978-1-5064-8040-4
Printed in Canada

This book was written on the land of the Massachusett people, who, despite European colonization, continue to survive today, passing on their rich tradition and knowledge through dance, drumming, storytelling, and other rituals. For more about the Massachusett, visit their website at massachusetttribe.org.

For my parents, Matthew and Christine,
who shared with me their deep love of poetry,
prose, and God, as well as their conviction that
we are here to use both our struggles and our
gifts to help others.

Contents

CONTENTS

CONTENTS

CONTENTS

CONTENTS

CONTENTS

CONTENTS

PREFACE

Most of these poems and meditations were written during a global pandemic. A pandemic is not the same as depression, but as someone who has now gone through both, I can tell you that the isolation, fear, grief, powerlessness, and uncertainty can feel very similar. You don't enter into either one by choice. You are isolated, yet more dependent on others than you want to be. You don't know what's happening at first, and you don't know how bad it will be or how long it will last. There are so many experts and opinions, but really there is no roadmap. You have to figure out how you're going to make it through just by waking up every day and figuring out that day.

Back before the pandemic started, in October of 2019, I started writing poems in the evenings on Twitter. I liked the structure that Twitter's 280-character limit imposed. I started most poems with the word "peace" and looked into my own heart and mind to name what I was struggling with, or thinking about, or needing peace for that day. I knew from years of blogging and being on social media, as well as writing a book, that the more personal and honest I was about my own struggles, the more people would say to me, "Me too. I feel that way, too. I thought I was the only one."

Those evening poems would eventually become my book *365 Days of Peace: Benedictions to End Your Day in Gentleness and Hope*. But before I self-published *365 Days*, I brought the idea to Broadleaf Books, the publishers of my first book, *The Long Night: Readings and Stories to Help You through Depression*. They liked the idea, but suggested that I focus on a more specific audience. They suggested it be the same audience as *The Long Night*, people struggling with depression and those who love them. And they challenged me to vary the form more, to step away from my starting place of "peace" and find other ways into honesty, poetry, and connection. I thought those were both great ideas.

So in a sense, it is as if my first two books had a baby and the book you're holding in your hand is the result. You can totally read it on its own, but if you've read either of my first two, you'll recognize themes from both of them. A handful of my favorite "peace" poems have made their way into it as well. If you're new here, welcome; I've tried to make the new folks feel at home. And if you've found your way here from *The Long Night* or *365 Days*, or both, thank you for coming back. It means more to me than I can say.

Another thing depression and living through a pandemic have in common is that they can both steal your ability to concentrate. When I'm going through a major depression, I lose my ability to get lost in a good book, to do well in my studies, even to follow the plot of a movie. In *The Long Night*, I tried to keep my chapters short, knowing that many of my readers would struggle to manage large chunks of text. In this book, I've gone even shorter, offering mostly one-page poems and meditations for those who need connection and reassurance but can't focus on a complicated thought or story. And if you aren't struggling with concentration, still I hope the shorter format will help you slow down just a little. Think of each poem as an invitation to take a deep breath, to unclench your muscles, and to set aside the stress of the day, just for a moment.

***

When I wrote a proposal for *The Long Night*, it included this description:

"This book is for those who are in the long night of waiting. It does not promise healing or deliverance, it is not a guide to praying away the depression. It is just an attempt to sit next to you while you wait, to let you know that you are not alone, that this time will not last forever."

The artist who designed the book's cover, Olga Grlic, zeroed in on the phrase, "You are not alone, and this will not last forever," and printed it in the full moon—a beacon of assurance and hope against the dark blue background of a starry night sky. By the time the book was published in May 2020,

COVID-19 had shut down schools and restaurants, mask-wearing had become a political shibboleth, and we were beginning to realize that this was going to last longer than a few weeks. I started tweeting the words from my book cover daily: "You are not alone, and this will not last forever." Many people assumed I was referring to the pandemic, and I was, though I was also speaking to those with depression, and especially to the dear souls who had to struggle through both simultaneously.

Sometimes when I tweeted those words people asked anxiously for reassurance—"Do you promise?" Other times people expressed disbelief, or even anger, feeling like the words were empty or meaningless. Sometimes I felt bad about tweeting the words out of context, as if I were ignoring the isolation and the deep pain and grief we were all feeling.

But here's what I meant, and what I mean: When I write, "You are not alone," I mean that even though everything you're experiencing is unique to your dear, beloved heart, it is also part of the depth of human experience. As Terence wrote, "I am human, and nothing human is alien to me." And I mean that although we may be physically isolated, by illness or by distance, we need each other. You are needed—you have something unique and beautiful to offer the world. And your own needs are not too much, but rather are part of what binds you to others in community.

And when I write, "This will not last forever," I don't mean that everything will be fine, that the future is rosy, that pain will disappear. I mean that this specific time will not last forever. Something will shift. There will be pain in the future, too, but there will also be joy. You are not stuck in this moment forever.

A Note on the Seasons Structure

In this book I use the seasons autumn, winter, and spring to represent the cycle of a depressive episode, its beginning, middle, and end. I could have used evening, night, and morning to go along with the theme of depression as a long night, but I chose to go with seasons, to add another layer of metaphor and to explore the relationship of our bodies and minds to the planet we live on, to nature and its cycles. So the seasons are metaphors in one sense, but literal in another. The light, the temperature, the colors of the leaves or bare branches, the behavior of the animals— even holed up in our homes we are connected to all that goes on in tree and burrow, sea and sky.

A NOTE ON THE SEASONS STRUCTURE

We have forgotten how tied we are to nature, but our bodies remember and respond to the seasons with shifting mood and energy. Can you feel the earth breathing around you? See the sky with its ever-shifting cloudscape? Hear the birds and the wind in the trees? Ground your feet in the same soil that nourishes the food you eat? Touch your own soft animal skin? We are part of the earth, part of all the life it holds. And that, too, is a way in which we're not alone.

You are not alone,
and this will not last forever.

PART I

AUTUMN

You expected to be sad in the fall. Part of you died each year when the leaves fell from the trees and their branches were bare against the wind and the cold, wintery light. But you knew there would always be the spring...

~ Ernest Hemingway, *A Moveable Feast*

You see, one loves the sunset when one is so sad.

~ Antoine de Saint-Exupéry, *The Little Prince*

Autumn is the season when it begins. The nights lengthen, the days become cold and crisp, the leaves blaze bright and then fall, thousands of tiny losses crunching under your feet. In the same way, depression comes both suddenly and slowly—one day your heart fills with joy at the bright orange maple trees, the next they might as well be wet-cement gray for all the power they have to stir emotion out of your dull, heavy heart. Depression comes, sometimes literally in the autumn as our bodies react to the fading light with seasonal affective disorder, but sometimes it comes in the middle of the summer, when everyone else seems to be outside in the sunshine, laughing, running, playing, while inside your mind the sun has set and the shadows have lengthened and taken over.

Autumn is my favorite season, even though winter is always hard. I wonder how much the beauty of the fall is enhanced by the knowledge that soon things will get hard, that soon life will be heavier. Some winters are harder than others, but you don't know what kind of year it will be when the first frost tinges the morning grass. You only know that your heart is saying goodbye to a certain light and lightness that you won't see again for a long time. You know, too, that spring will come, that warmth and joy will return. But in between is winter, that long night of the earth, that long night of the soul.

Don't worry, reader. We'll walk through it together.

Invocation

This poem is a prayer for you
my mind shapes these words
for you, my fingers find the keys
clicking them harder than is strictly
        necessary.

This book is a prayer for you
this paper, or this screen, contains secrets
only you can read.

This stanza is a prayer for you
this line lingers near your bedside
this one makes the sign of a cross
this one lights a candle
this one cries out the ache
        in my heart for you

Dear friend, reader, fellow sufferer
if you have forgotten how to pray
I will remind you:

Touch your own soft palm
to your own warm face

There. You have turned your body
into a prayer.

A Blessing for Seasonal Affective Disorder

Peace to those who are nervous
because this time last year
and many years before
depression paid a call

Peace to those whose bodies
and minds have trouble
adjusting to the fading light

Peace to those who have difficult memories
connected to this time of year

Tonight may peace be yours, and strength
to ground you through the long nights.

THE DEATH OF LEAVES

You are not the leaves
which blaze with color every fall, then fall
ground into the ground.

Their death is not your death.

No, you are the tree, which moves its energy
down in autumn, to the roots, in ample store.
Bare branches best prepared
for winter cold and winter winds.

That's not to say the loss of leaves is not a loss.
The grief of losing all your color, your
        connection to the sun
is real grief. The stripping is a real stripping.

But as every fall speaks of coming spring
and every winter holds its end in its beginning
your own sap will rise again in longer light
nourishing every small branch
and you, tree, human, living creature
will grow green life again.

A Blessing for November

Here in New England, October's foliage
is over-the-top gorgeous every year.

So much so that Edna St. Vincent Millay
begged God for mercy from such beauty.

November is much more humble.
Earthy. Its colors more subdued

And then there is the end of daylight savings—
that plunge into darkness.

May that darkness be a place we
meet each other this year

May the quiet of those extended nights
be where we learn to hear God's voice

and maybe even, finally,
our own.

What I Mean by Prayer

I'm writing this as a prayer for you
but what do I mean by prayer
when the words I used to pray
have turned to sand in my mouth?

I mean I know you are trying
as hard as you can
(maybe too hard).

I mean that I know you are in pain
and the pain is not your fault.

I believe you.

I am with you.

And I mean, too, that God knows
you are trying as hard as you can
(maybe too hard).

God knows you are in pain
and the pain is not your fault.

God believes you.

God is with you.

WARM AND COLD
WATER I

Be a little gentler
　　with your
　　　　self
　　the world is
　　　　　　hard enough
　　　　and only you
　　have
　　　　access to the
　　　　　　valve inside
　　　　　　　　your head
　　　　　　that turns
　　　　warm/cold
　　　　　　　water
　　　　warm/cold
　　thoughts
　　　　on
　　and
　　　　off.

THE GOOD NIGHT

Now the good night
settles in softly
puts her arms around you
and says,

Love,
you do not have to smile
or cheer up

Put on a brave face
or soldier on

Fake it till you make it
or hold it together
anymore.

I'm here
and it is time
to rest.

WHEN IT BEGINS

I've seen fall leaves here in Boston as early as late July. Just a little one, a spot of red on an otherwise green sugar maple. My last major depressive episode started that way. Days were still fine, but in the evenings I had these little glimpses of inexplicable sadness that were gone by morning. It wasn't fall yet, but fall was coming.

Now I know what to watch for. I've lived in New England long enough to know that it's the sugar maples you have to keep an eye on. Unlike autumn, depressive episodes can be caught in time and often prevented. You check in with your doctor, maybe tweak your meds, enact all your hard-learned coping mechanisms. But sometimes depression comes anyway, and then it helps to remember that you've made it through the fall and winter before. At least this time you don't feel the same shock you felt before. At least this time you know that autumn carries with it the promise of spring.

*You are not alone in what
you're going through.*

BLESSED ARE THE OVERTHINKERS

Blessed are the overthinkers
for they are never for a moment in danger
of living an unexamined life.

Blessed are the empaths
for they understand many
perspectives different than their own.

Blessed are those who have been sick
for they are the only ones who know
what health really means.

Blessed are you when you are misunderstood
for you will one day be the only one
to understand someone else

And that may truly save a life.

SOMEONE KNOWS WHAT YOU MEAN

At this very moment,
someone is feeling the exact thing you are
feeling,
The thing that makes you feel so ashamed
and so isolated.

Someone has felt this exact kind of loneliness
before
this sickening hopelessness
this festering boredom
this paralyzing fear of everything and nothing.

Someone will feel it again in the future
and will need to know
that you have felt it, too.

You are never alone.

A Prayer for Lost Things

Peace to the things you've lost over the years
your grey sweater, eight years ago in Maine
the other blue earring, at the park last summer
countless socks, countless places
a book left on the train to New York in June.

A job, more than one job,
an old love, or two, or three
a once-dear friend, now grown apart
a whole community, now grown apart
your childhood pet
your adulthood pet
your loved ones.

Peace to the holding on and the letting go.
Peace to moving forward, but not on.

A REGIFTING

There is a line of scripture
which says that three things remain
    faith,
    hope,
    and love
But those words can lose their meaning
    when all we feel is dullness and despair.

So let's give them back to each other.

Let faith mean we believe each other's pain.

Let hope mean we have given up hope
    and keep breathing anyway.

Let love mean we don't remember
    the joy of love, but we keep showing up.

I am here. Love means we are here.

And so our presence with each other proves
    that you and I are loved.

A Prayer for the Shortening Days

Welcome, darkness, and the coming cold.

Welcome, lamplight, candlelight, and firelight.

Welcome, long, dark evenings and late dawns.

Welcome, slower pace and slower energy.

Welcome to every feeling in my heart, my spirit, and my body

whether pleasant, painful, or complicated.

I make room for you.

I make room for my full self.

In gentleness

And in hope.

LIVE TO FIGHT ANOTHER DAY

What if someone looked at you
   compassionately
while you kicked and raged, and said,
"Dear one, you seem tired and hungry.

"Here is a snack. I will keep guard while
   you eat,
stave off the demons while you rest."

What if you said that to yourself?

Don't worry—I'm not saying you have to
   stop worrying.
I know you can't. But you can catch up on
   worrying later.
Feed yourself. Lay your body down gently.

Let your angel-self stand guard for an hour
over your precious animal-self, who needs
nourishment, care, grooming, rest.

Hold off the demons for a little while
and return to the battle fresh.

Live, in other words, live
to fight another day.

A Blessing for Turning the Clocks Back

Blessed be the evenings
that begin, now, in the afternoon
the hours and hours of lamplight before bed

Blessed be the blinking stove lights
the car dashboards, the secret codes
we must know to adapt to this new normal

Blessed be the dark bedtimes
and the wakenings that have
borrowed this shrinking daylight
but will soon be dark themselves

Blessed be the darkness itself
our teacher and just possibly this year
our friend.

Others have traveled this road before,
have felt this pain before.

EMBODIED BLESSING

May you be blessed and kept
held in the arms of something
soft and warm, something strong.

This God that blesses you
turns their face upon you
but also their strong back

To carry you, arms
to hold you or help you
lift the weight of this day

A soft stomach where you
can pillow your head
warm flesh, for God became flesh

May you find graciousness and strength for
the day
and peace and gentleness for the long night.

SPIRAL STAIRCASE

I know it is excruciatingly hard to find
yourself
in the same bad place again
With the same depression, same fears
same hopelessness as before

But look closer.

This is not a circle, but a spiral staircase.
From a certain view it seems that you
are going around in circles

But shift your perspective and you realize
you are so much higher than before
ready to face these feelings and this
     circumstance
with more wisdom, more hard-won
     experience
more coping mechanisms in place.

And when you circle back again next time
you will have even more, and be even
further
with even more evidence
that you can make it through.

THE CALM AFTER A STORM

You may have done everything right—
worked hard
swallowed your pride
stayed in your lane, hydrated
taken your meds and still

The day unraveled around you.

Some days just do.

And then there is nothing left to do
but to give in to the unraveling
and to the deep and tired calm
that only comes after a storm.

LAST TIME

The last time you were here
you felt so alone.
I did, too.

But if you recognize in these pages
the fear, the gut-sinking hopelessness
the feeling of falling into a deep pit without
handholds
the bleakness of another coming winter

Then you'll know I've felt the way you feel
and I'll know you've felt what I feel
and neither you nor I
need ever feel
so alone
again

A Blessing for the Heart

Today I anoint with oil
your righteous anger.

I sprinkle holy water over
your body's wholly justified fear
of leaving the house without armor.

I bless your inexplicable sadness
and your very specific sadness.

I ordain your emotions
to be sacred ministers
of truth
and of grace.

A Friendship

What if there is actually no way
to go through life without challenges,
heartbreak, and pain

And the choices you made
were as good as any other?

Why don't we let our
younger selves off the hook
today?

Blame the consequences
on the consequences

And be friends.

A Safe Place to Live

My body is soft and warm
like a beach, like soil

I am an earth unto myself
a safe place to live, to breathe

My legs root, stabilize emotions
arms hold and rock my troubled mind

Flesh soothes spirit
skin comforts soul

Peace, my body says
I am here, you are whole.

EPIGRAPHS

Be kind, everyone

you meet is fighting

a great battle.

Everyone fighting a great battle

is met by you, one way or another.

When you are fighting a great battle

you will likely meet some unkind people.

The great battle is to meet so many

people who want to fight

and still be kind.

TIDAL PRAYER

I used to, in disasters,
try to account for everyone I loved

Are we okay?

Let us be okay.

But now I love too many people
and the world is full of disasters

so I pray

By opening my heart wide
letting it fill with all my pain and love

And emptying it into the sea
to be borne again
by the tide.

You Will Be Sustained

Maybe today will be the day things turn around, the day you find what you've been looking for, the supposed key to happiness, the missing link. Maybe it will be just cold enough to rouse you to the beauty of the orange trees against the blue sky, or the soft touch of the brown-eyed toddler that woke you up way too early. Or maybe it will be another day of plodding through life doing the best you can, trying to pay the bills, take care of the ones that you know you used to love before this fog settled into your brain and your heart, watching the clock count the minutes till you can move on to the next task, till you can eat another meal, till you can sleep.

Maybe you are aware of the tremendous, universe-sustaining love of God, and maybe you have lost even the tiny glimmer of a sense of God's presence. Either way, breathe deep. Breathe the frosty morning air into every part of your body. God is as close as your breath, as all-surrounding and ever-present. Maybe today won't be the day that you finally feel awake, alive, and loved. But you will be, whether you feel it or not. And every breath, pulled in and pushed out into wispy steam, every breath you take is proof that you will be sustained, today and every day, God in you, God around you, God before you and behind. Breathe deep.

Lower and Deeper

You don't have to know how to pray
to pray
You only have to notice your thoughts
and let them go
or not be able to let them go.

But prayer goes on just the same
somewhere in your belly
lower and deeper than
the thin altitude of
anxious analysis.

Prayer breathes for you
your breath prays for you
your mind participates only
by observing, resting

Occasionally making its
presence known with a word:
"Yes" will do, or "peace"
but an entire diatribe
will only float above the prayer

then fade like a cloud
on a rainless day.

Welcome

Welcome to this page, today, tonight, this morning.

Welcome to those who have faith
and to those who don't.

Welcome to those who had to choose
between loving the God they were sold
and loving themselves,
and chose themselves.

Welcome to those
whose love of God
lets them love others enough
to trust their choice.

Welcome to those
who are still learning this trust.

COMPLICATIONS I

Comorbidity is the presence of two or more conditions occurring in a person, either at the same time, or successively (one condition that occurs right after the other). Conditions described as comorbidities are often long-term (chronic) conditions.

~ Sherry Christiansen

What I want to say here
is that depression is hard enough
and I'm so sorry you have to go through
all of that other pain
as well as this deep pain.

And I see you.
And I believe you.
And it's not your fault.
And you are doing the
damn well best you can.

A BLESSING FOR THE LONELY

A blessing for the lonely tonight. For those alone in their bed who never shared their bed, and for those whose bedmate is newly gone.

A blessing for those alone in their house who live alone, for those who live with people they're not close to, for those who lived with children who now live elsewhere, and for those whose children no longer live.

A blessing for those alone in a crowd: in their place of worship or in their community, or even in a group of friends yet still feeling alone.

A blessing for the lonely who withdraw on purpose, and one for those who reach out again and again yet still feel alone.

A blessing for those surrounded by love who don't know how to feel loved, and so still feel alone.

A blessing for the ones who are lonely and say so, so that others will feel less alone in their loneliness.

A blessing for you. You are seen. You are known. You are loved.

AN UNOBSTRUCTED STREAM

I have started to let sadnesses visit whenever they come, because I know that trying to keep them out will just cause them to find another, more aggressive way in.

~ Jonny Sun, *Goodbye, Again*

The other day I took the kids I nanny to one of my favorite spots in the woods, where a stream runs down a hillside and under a bridge on the footpath. We played "Pooh Sticks" for a while, dropping sticks off one side of the bridge, and waiting for them to emerge on the other side. After a while I noticed that a lot of the sticks were getting stuck on a build-up of leaves and branches under the bridge, so the kids and I found long branches and set about cleaning out the gunk, experimenting with different angles to see which gave us the best reach and view of the obstruction.

Our tears and sorrow—along with our anger, frustration, fear, and confusion—are like that stream. If we allow them to be, they flow smoothly, and the feelings pass through us. But if they get caught up in the debris of guilt or blame, or of being diminished by others or by us, they cause a blockage that builds and builds, and they end up staying with us, affecting our mental and physical health. We have to take time to let ourselves feel our own very specific sadness as well as the general sadness of the world, knowing that in the end it will be less painful than if we ignore it. And we have to let others feel what they feel, too, and acknowledge their feelings.

That day in the woods I begged off of our work on the stream after a while, and leaned back against a tree as the kids kept working, following the stream farther up the hill, leaping from bank to bank. I watched them, trying not to be nervous about them falling, or falling in. That's part of childhood, after all—falling down, getting muddy and wet, letting the tears come, and then getting back up again to play. When they do fall, I say, "Oh, that looked like it hurt! Can I see? Any blood? Do you need a hug?"

What if we gave ourselves the attention and care we would give to a child? What if we looked at our pain and acknowledged it? What if we showed it to someone we trusted and said, "This hurts. I'm bleeding." And what if we offered acknowledgment to each other of that pain? "That does look like it hurts. I'm sorry. Do you need a hug, or a prayer, or maybe just for me to sit on the other end of the phone while you cry? I'm here."

THINGS YOU CAN SURVIVE

You do not have a fatal flaw.

Listen to me.

You do not have a fatal flaw.

You make mistakes—
That is survivable.

Your body has needs—
They can be filled.

You can't seem to fit in—
This will not lead to death.

You need to be loved—
There is enough love to live on.

You are stubborn—
This may even save your life.

You are sometimes weak—
Others will help carry you.

You are loud—
You will not die of it
(and no one else will die of it).

Believe me. You do not have a fatal flaw.
You are not doomed to be your own
undoing.

THRIVING

You have been fighting for so long just to
survive
Just to make it through another day
To pay the bills
To get better

What would it look like for you to thrive?

What would it look like to have a life
filled with purpose and joy?

What would you need to change?

Maybe all of that seems
like an impossible dream right now
but a day will come when suddenly you
realize

There is a path towards that dream
and you take one faltering step forward

And until then, the dream of thriving
might help you to survive.

Can you feel us here with you,
waiting for something to shift?

Monsters under the Bed

Peace to those who are afraid tonight
anxious, worried, terrified

Those who know in their bones
that there are monsters under the bed
despite what the grownups say

Peace to those who shake
and weep but do all that grownups
have to do anyway

Peace to those
who cannot.

Just Breaking Even

I know you are hoping
things get a little better today
just ease up a tiny bit, that's all

I know you wake hopeful
and go to sleep discouraged again
and only want some small sign

That it's two steps forward
to each step back
and some days, honestly
just breaking even
would be a mercy.

Hold on.

I promise,

this will not last forever.

ANOTHER DAILY DISASTER

I see you.

You who were just getting your feet back
under you
when disaster struck

Maybe a small, commonplace disaster
but enough to ruin sleep
raise blood pressure
shift things from almost okay
to not okay at all.

It was just when you thought you had
a little breathing room wasn't it?

Just then.

I see you, now
struggling to breathe
through another daily disaster.

Part II
Winter

In the middle of winter I at last discovered that there was in me an invincible summer.

~ Albert Camus, "Return to Tipasa"

Winter is the middle, when the depression has settled in and you realize it's going to be more than a quick fix. Some people speak of winter's darkness, and it's true that winter nights are long, but contrary to what you may have been taught, darkness in and of itself is not wrong or evil. Darkness is a necessary space between days and summers, a space where we can rest, a space that has its own beauty and its own wisdom. But depression is different. Depression is slate gray where there should be color. Depression is a pit with sheer sides and no discernable handholds. Depression is not the rich, potent darkness of soil, or the stillness of night when you can finally hear your own voice, and maybe even God's. Depression is asphalt. Depression is emptiness with no hope of being filled. Depression is winter, when you have lost sight of the fall and cannot imagine the spring.

But winter is a time of renewal, too. Winter is a time of rest, of hibernation, a time of slowing down. And as long and hard as it may be, it holds its own ending within itself. The first day of winter is the longest night of the year, and every day after marks an earlier sunrise and a later sunset than the day before. January skies are brighter than December skies, and February even more so. The winter may be long, but it will not last forever. It never does.

Winter Solstice

Did you know that the first day of winter
is when the days stop getting shorter
and your hemisphere begins to climb
toward light and life again?

So exactly the moment when winter
begins
it also begins to end.
Just when things feel the bleakest
is when they can turn around at any
moment

Or, to put it another way
as my dear friend Laura says,
"Hopelessly lost and nearly found
feel exactly the same."

Hold on.

MORE LIFE, NOT LESS

I used to think that depression
meant that life was too much
and I needed less of it.

Discouraged in spirit
weak and weary in body.

But this weariness is not too-bright life.
It is the shadow of death.

And death cannot overcome death.
Only life can.

More life
More rest
More tenderness
More hot meals
More cool breezes

More honest tears
More caring friends
More life-saving medicine and medication

More life
Not less.

Sparks

In each of us there is a spark of the divine
and we must work to release this spark
to join into a great, holy fire.

You may not be the next Van Gogh
Yo-Yo Ma, Angelou, or DuVerney

But the world needs you
just as much as it needed them.

No matter how bad the depression is
that spark remains in you

And all the other flames
yearn for it.

Without you we cannot be whole
Without each one of you

I cannot
fully
ignite.

A Blessing for the Body

Today I anoint with oil
your whole, good body.

I sprinkle holy water over
muscles, bones, sinew
your strong inner core.

I bless your vital layer of fat
and your soft, warm skin.

I ordain your eyes, ears, and mouth
to be sacred ministers
of love, of truth
and of grace.

THE DEAD OF WINTER

It feels so close to death here
everything bitter cold,
                brittle cold
where fingers and hearts uncovered
                go numb.

But this winter is not unto death.
This is not a sinking into the grave

        it is a burrowing

                deeper into the rich earth,

        a storing

                of warmth in soft hair,

                soft fur.

And every creature curled in sleep

every tulip bulb

and buried seed

and you and I

carry, faithful and flickering,

our own

tiny sun.

A Blessing for Stillness

Be still and know
that there is no knowledge or
lack of knowledge

That can separate you from God
or make any of this all right.

Be still and know
that you may never know
the reason for this suffering.

Be still and know
that you do not have to know why
in order to find peace.

Be still and let the stillness
be its own knowledge.

ANOTHER INVITATION

Come for a walk with me, my friend...Come into the whis-
pering darkness of the trees at twilight and listen to the
scripture they speak. Come into the shadows of the oaks and
lindens until the darkness outside matches the darkness in
your soul. Then listen to how the dark speaks its own lan-
guage, one you could not hear in the bright light of day.

~ From *The Long Night,* "Invitation"

I asked you, once, to come for a walk with
me
and you did, we walked together
through the strange twilight world
with which we were both familiar.

That westering world, that night
you thought you'd leave quickly
when you first arrived. You thought

There must be an easy path
over or around or even through it—
this could not be the way things were.

Now you are here again, or maybe
meeting me for the first time.

I won't ask you to walk.

Just sit by me for a while
and I'll sit by you
so that both of us know
we are not alone.

WHEN IT SEEMS LIKE IT WILL NEVER END

Every December and into January I think I'm doing all right. Sure, winter is cold, my skin brittle from the dry air and pale from lack of sun. Sure, my once-curly hair lies flat and staticky across my cheeks, and the mid-afternoon darkness feels like tangible weight, like sodden clothing. But I track the sunsets daily, every evening after December twenty-first brings one minute more light, and I lean into the metaphor of darkness, the stillness where I can meet God and myself in a way the brightness of summer doesn't permit.

Then February hits.

And suddenly it has always been winter and it will always be winter and I am broken in my bed as the radiators clank out too much heat and my throat hurts from it. Sometimes depression is like that. When it begins it's awful, but you rally and see your doctor and your therapist and your yoga instructor, and pray prayers of welcome and acceptance, and remember that it will eventually pass, and think you're doing okay. And then suddenly you're not at the beginning anymore, and nowhere near the end, and it feels like you've just been here, in the middle of it all, forever.

This is when it's most important to hold on. Just breathe. Just breathe. Just breathe. March is on its way.

THE RELEASE OF TEARS

Peace to those who cannot think
or even really feel
peace to the numb.

Peace to those whose fear and anger
never goes away anymore
even in sleep.

Peace to those who can't stop crying
and to those who would give anything
for the release of tears.

Peace to all your brave hearts tonight.

We need you.
We're not complete without you.

Signs of Life

There was a time when you could
laugh and run, and the laughter was
the same as the running.

That was happiness, I think.
But now something rests on top of you.
What is it? It holds you down.

I think of that weight as a tiger
malevolent, huge, blinking as it paws me
with the smugness of believing

That it could kill me anytime.
But I catch glimpses of proof
that you and I are stronger—

We haven't given up,
for one. That's strength
unimaginable

And, look, I am writing
and you are reading
which are sure signs
        of life.

BE A MOTHER TO YOUR BODY

Your mind may not remember
the intensity of the pain
but your flesh does

Let it feel what it feels.
Be a mother to your body

Rock her gently
stroke her hair

Tell her, *I know, love.*
I know it hurts. I'm here.

She will not stop crying
because of your ministrations
but her tears will finally be

The release
they were always
meant to be.

A Lament for the Weary

A lament for the weary:
those whose bones depression has rusted
though on the surface it may be barely
noticeable.

Those who swallow Advil or Lexapro
and make it through the day
but collapse at night.

Those who have waited
almost their whole lives just to feel okay
and are waiting still.

We see you, we who are rusting.

We see you, we who are swallowing.

We see you, we who are waiting.

We will wait with you.

COMMUNITY

Maybe you'll be in a place
to help someone today

or maybe you'll have to ask for help
for the *nth* day in a row.

Maybe you'll be someone's comfort
or maybe you'll need their comfort.

It's not a numbers game, it's community
and you're a part of it.

You belong
you're needed
we need you.

WHAT THE ANGELS WONDER

Angels fear to tread these paths, Beloved
but you and I, we have no fear of either
God or demons

God having already laid us this low
and our demons so familiar, if not friends.

Nothing can scare you
when you have lived forever in a state of
disaster.

Angels wonder how we manage
with our flesh so prone to pain

Hearts so broken and broken again
before the first break can heal.

Spirits—yes, they understand spirits
but this crushing of spirits, no, nor this
fluttering hope.

Angels long to look into these things
as we long to soar above them.

But what they know only in theory
we must live to learn in our bodies:

That as Rumi said, the cure for the pain
is in the pain. So we breathe (and angel
wings fan oxygen)
and we hurt and breathe and hurt, again.

THE NIGHTINGALE

Traditionally a nightingale is a symbol of intense love, felt by the bird for the rose. For the Sufi, the yearning soul is the nightingale, God himself the rose.

~ Sister Wendy Beckett

One night I stayed at Churchill's villa in Morocco, and as I lay shivering under heavy blankets, a bird sang a song sweeter than any I'd ever heard before. In the morning our language teacher told us it was the only time in his seventy years he'd heard a nightingale, and I shivered again with the honor of eavesdropping on this old man's sacred gift, when I was, myself, still young. That was also the trip I realized I was too sick to travel anymore, unless something changed. Too worn out with foot pain to walk the streets of Marrakesh, too weary with migraines to lean into hours of conversation in another tongue, my mental health too dependent on routine and easy access to friends and family to be so many oceans and mountains from home.

It was a hard, sad trip in many ways, and a hard, sad, realization.

But still there was the nightingale.

Promise I

Today may be hard and sad

but there will be at least one beautiful
thing in it.

Maybe it will be a nightingale

singing outside your window at midnight

or a humble sparrow at dawn

Maybe it will be a good nap

a call from a friend

or an unexpected belly laugh at the
weirdest thing

Pay attention.

Promise II

If you don't see anything beautiful today

that means it's coming tomorrow

or the day after

Soon

or

eventually

There will be beauty again.

Hold on.

You are not alone,
so I am not alone, either.

WOUNDED HEALERS

Peace to the wounded healers
who use their pain
to help others—
To those who listen.

Peace to the prophets whose word
burns within them but disappears
into the noise of the world
when spoken.

Peace to the wound.

Peace to the healing.

Peace to the word.

Peace to the hearing.

YOU ARE BELOVED

I am my beloved's and my beloved is mine.

~ Song of Songs 10:6 NIV

God has been saying from all eternity, 'You are my beloved.'
From all eternity, before we were born, we existed in the
mind of God. God loved us before our fathers and mothers
loved us.

~ Henri Nouwen

I am my beloved's and my beloved is mine

I am not alone, I am loved

I am loved, I am love, I am beloved

You are your beloved's and your beloved
is yours

You are never alone

Even when you are alone, you are the
Beloved

Your name is Beloved.

IMAGINE GOD

Imagine God up there and you down here
Now imagine God with you, God
curled up on your lap, humming a lullaby.
Imagine God stroking your hair as you cry
or you stroking God's.

Imagine a distant God, checking God's
watch
waiting for you to pray.
Now imagine instead God slipping off
your watch
setting it on your nightstand
as you roll over in your sleep.

Imagine sleep as God, imagine waking as
forgetting God
and trying all day to remember what
caused
that fading, delicious feeling of finally
being
with someone who deeply loves you.

Now imagine
that it's true.

A BLESSING FOR
THE MIND

Today I anoint with oil
your tired mind.

I sprinkle holy water over
your thoughts that spin in circles
and your thoughts that have been stuck for days.

I bless your wondering, your questions and
the answers you settle on, for a time or for
always.

I ordain your imagination and your creativity
to be sacred ministers
of love, of truth
and of grace.

SPEAK SOFTLY TO YOUR BODY

Be gentle with yourself today.

Offer your heart kindness and grace.

Speak softly to your body
brush your own hair back from your face
call yourself sweetheart.

Laugh at your own jokes
be amazed at your wit and creativity.

Allow all your feelings space.

YOUR FOREIGN TONGUE

Be patient toward all that is unsolved in your heart and try to love the questions themselves, like locked rooms and like books that are now written in a very foreign tongue.

~ Rainer Maria Rilke

Before you can read the story of your life
you have to learn the language.
Luckily, you are your own dictionary,
so pay attention.

Your heart will teach you the adjectives—
bright, joyful, yellow
despairing, foggy, blue—

Your mind the nouns of you—
bed, nightstand, medications
door, friends, outside—

Your body tells you the words for the verbs—
sleep, wake, try
stretch, walk, dream—

And your spirit will know the adverbs—
hopelessly, slowly, surely
sometimes, almost, always.

A TRUE VOICE

The moment Jesus came up out of the baptismal waters, the skies opened up and he saw God's Spirit—it looked like a dove—descending and landing on him. And along with the Spirit, a voice: "This is my Son, chosen and marked by my love, delight of my life."

~ Matthew 3:17, *The Message* by Eugene Peterson

The moment you came up out of sleep this morning
the skies opened up, and something else opened, too,
something that crinkled ugly static like a broken radio.

The moment your mind came to consciousness
you could hear voices, and they were not all doves.

You could hear voices that were serpents,
goblins, trolls
telling you things about yourself no one
should hear or say.

They were lying.

But quieter, far above or far below those
voices
like a dove from heaven or the murmur of
an underground spring

A Voice told the truth, to you and about
you:
"This is my Beloved, the one I love
the joy and delight of my life."

How to Say "I Love You" to Someone Who Is Depressed I

"I am not going anywhere."

"You are worth more than your accomplishments."

"I believe you are doing the best you can."

"What do you need?"

"You are important to me."

"We need you here."

"Your needs are valid."

"If you want to talk, I will listen."

"It's okay if you want to be alone, but I am here when you need me."

"I believe you."

Everything shifts, eventually.

OUR OWN DEAR FRIEND

Are you one of us? We who flinch
when we look in the mirror?
Whose eyes have been trained
to see our flesh as flawed?

And yet see how our body,
our own dear friend,
is always there for us.

Always soft, always welcoming
our minds to indwell.

Anytime to sink
into depth of belly, skin, and hair
the peace and safety of our warm,
animal self.

Repent of Repenting

Repent
of repenting.

Just for now, let your thoughts pass by
without critique.

Let your body speak, for once,
its language of softness and warmth.

See what your heart actually says
when you're not daily insisting
that it has been deceitful.

See if your breath is not enough to make you
human and holy.

Love yourself as you would love others.

Let your self
be loved.

FOR THE END OF A REALLY HARD WINTER

I worry that we hunkered down so hard
those long, lonely nights

That even with spring's return
our bodies have rusted
in that defensive pose

How was it that we used to laugh
and stretch out languorously
in the generous evening light?

Like this?

Was it like this?

Will we remember?

We are not alone,
and this will not last forever.

Sunrise and Sunset

The sun rises with birdsong
calling gently to each of us
to breathe leaf-blessed oxygen
and give back that breath
to bird, to tree
to each other.

If sunrise is too bright
for you right now
keep breathing—soon enough
sunset will come with its
firm insistence
of our limitations

All creatures,
it will say,
must rest.

May the Memory Be a Blessing

Maybe today you can't remember
the feel of the sun on your face
even though the sun is on your face.

Or the way your heart used to lift
when you heard the birds sing
even though they are still singing.

Maybe right now you can't access
the feel of a gentle touch on your arm
even though your lover is still
holding you.

But you did, once.

May the memory be a promise
that those things still exist
and will return to you.

Love and joy will return.
Wait for them.

(I know the memory now is torture, too
but may it be a blessing. May it be a
blessing.)

THE PARTING GLASS

for Steve

But since it fell unto my lot
That I should rise and you should not
I'll gently rise and I'll softly call,
'Goodnight, and joy be with you all.'

> ~ "The Parting Glass," traditional Scottish song

Raise a glass, of water or of wine
to those who are alive today
though they might not have been.

Those who have survived illness or accident
or not-accident

Those who are glad to be alive,
and those only here grudgingly

And, oh! raise a glass to those
who could not come to terms with life

And to all of us who have to go on here
without them.

THE SUN WILL BREAK THROUGH

Peace to those with long-term depression
who want to believe that this will not
last forever, but have lost all sense of
time passing
here in this deep pit with sheer sides
buried in thick grey clouds.

Peace to the moment, some day

    I promise

        when the sun

will break through

    again

COMPLICATIONS II

Would I perhaps have been able to avoid altogether my experiences of depression? Would I have been whole instead of fragmented? Perhaps. I think, at the very least, that I would have had years of happiness that are now forever lost.

~ Andrew Solomon, on homophobia and internalized homophobia

What I want to say here
is that depression is hard enough
without the pain of homophobia
and the self-hatred and self-doubt
it engenders

And I see you
and I believe you
and I believe in you—

Your right to live and love
worship or not worship
raise a family or not raise a family
work and create art
fully and joyfully
without fear

And I'm so sorry for the times
that you couldn't.

PROPORTIONAL GRIEF

Grief is depression in proportion to circumstance; depression is grief out of proportion to circumstance.

~ Andrew Solomon, *The Noonday Demon: An Atlas of Depression*

Tell me the proportion of your grief.
Do you cry in the middle of the day
in the middle of movies?

Or do you wait
till the more appropriate end?

Tell me the proportion
of your depression.

Is it bigger than my fist?
Bigger than a loaf of bread?

Bigger than the cavity of your chest,
lungs filled or trying to fill?

Is your grief in its right and proper place
like water filling the sink and bathtub
Or is it dripping into pots and buckets
placed haphazardly throughout the house?

Is anything we feel
a proportionate response
to any of this?

Or have we all lost all sense
of proportion?

LOVE PERSEVERING

What is grief but love persevering?

~ WandaVision

If grief for the loss of someone you love
is love persevering

Then maybe depression is the love of everything

Love of this beautiful, broken world
love of your own precious life
love of the ideals you once held of love
before you were disappointed

Maybe depression is love out of proportion
to circumstances
Maybe depression is love trying to persevere
Maybe depression is life trying to persevere
against seemingly insurmountable odds

Maybe depression is life persevering.

WARM AND COLD WATER II

Be a little gentler
    with each
        other
the world is
        hard enough
    and you may
be one of the
    only ones
        who can
            reach the valve
                in someone's
            head
        that turns
warm/cold
        water
            warm/cold
thoughts
        on
and
        off.

A SMALL BOX

Beloved, I know you are worried tonight.

I know it's an ache that you feel

in your chest, your gut, your head.

I won't promise everything will be okay,
because everything's already not okay.

But I do promise that the bad thing won't
happen just because you didn't worry
about it enough.

Here's a small box.

Put your worry in here.

Close the lid.

And rest.

VALENTINE'S DAY FORECAST

The cold will be as bitter as unrequited
love—
biting, piercing, hopeless.

But, the sun. Oh! the sun,
though its rays seem to freeze and crumble
into ice crystals before they touch your
skin

Still, it will stretch out its arms and legs
like a just-waking child,
pushing back the night on both ends of the
day.

If you go out, despite your heartache
you won't be able to feel the skin on your
face.

But if you stay in, wear a sweater, and put
the kettle on
the sun will fill your house—the living
room at coffee time
and the kitchen for your late
afternoon tea—
with such a promise of love and warmth

    that the thermometer

will be helpless

    to deny.

Feel What We Feel

What if we gave ourselves the attention
and care
we would give to an injured child?
What if we looked at our pain and
acknowledged it?
What if we showed it to someone we
trusted and said,
"This hurts. I'm bleeding."

What if we offered each other
acknowledgment of that pain?

"That does look like it hurts."

"I'm sorry."

"Do you need a hug?"

What if, in other words,
we let each other and ourselves
feel the way we feel
and held ourselves and each other close
till we felt better enough
to keep going?

Winter will not last forever.

Part III
Spring

And soon Edmund noticed that the snow which splashed against them as they rushed through it was much wetter than it had been all last night. At the same time he noticed that he was feeling much less cold. It was also becoming foggy...There also seemed to be a curious noise all round them, but the noise of their driving and jolting and the dwarf's shouting at the reindeer prevented Edmund from hearing what it was, until suddenly the sledge stuck so fast that it wouldn't go on at all. When that happened there was a moment's silence. And in that silence Edmund could at last listen to the other noise properly. A strange, sweet, rustling, chattering noise—and yet not so strange, for he'd heard it before—if only he could remember where! Then all at once he did remember. It was the noise of running water. All round them though out of sight, there were streams, chattering, murmuring, bubbling, splashing and even (in the distance) *roaring. And his heart gave a great leap (though he hardly knew why) when he realized that the frost was over. And much nearer there was a drip-drip-drip from the branches of all the trees. And then, as he looked at one tree he saw a great load of snow slide off it and for the first time since he had entered Narnia he saw the dark green of a fir tree.*

~ C. S. Lewis, *The Lion, the Witch, and the Wardrobe*

"I thought you were dead! But then I thought I was dead myself. Is everything sad going to come untrue? What's happened to the world?"

"A great Shadow has departed," said Gandalf, and then he laughed and the sound was like music, or like water in a parched land; and as he listened the thought came to Sam that he had not heard laughter, the pure sound of merriment, for days upon days without count.

~ J. R. R. Tolkien, *The Return of the King*

If autumn is the beginning and winter is the middle, then spring is the end of the long night of depression. Not the end, rather, but a new beginning, a new glimpse of hope, a break in the seemingly endless ice and algor, the constantly running heat turning your skin as dry and frail as paper. The shift begins well into what we think of as winter, in February when the angle of the sunlight shifts and snow melts faster, even if the temperatures remain basically the same. The birds, too, begin to sing a different song in spring, a song of hope and expectation, of reproduction and birth and rebirth. If your depression is seasonal, or if it just happens to coincide with the seasons this year, you might feel your spirit lift with the birdsong, or the fresh breeze from a finally-opened window.

If your depression coincides with a pandemic, it might be the news of a new vaccine in March, or an appointment for the vaccine in April that breaks through the dullness and the pain. If your depression doesn't coincide with either, you may feel the warmth and sun as a bitter reminder that you are not well. It's okay. You are allowed to feel what you feel and heal on your own schedule. I am not here to urge you into premature celebration. But I will, gently, try to speak of spring and the end of a long suffering. I will try to remind you of the joy that birdsong once brought to your heart, that morning when you were young and you woke to the feel of something different in the air. I will try to describe the brightness of leaf buds, the return of green life that winter buried. And I will wait here for you, beside this babbling stream, ready to mourn while you mourn, but also to rejoice with you when your own great Shadow departs.

ALL OF US HERE

Out of everyone here, there are
those who found pockets of peace today
and those who could not.

Among us, there are
those whose hearts lifted
at the song of a bird from a newly opened window

And those who heard and closed the window
because the bird's joy was so at odds with our
sorrow.

Do you hear the birdsong right now, where
you are?

If you don't, it's okay.

Stay here with us.

We'll wait till you do.

ALL OF YOU

Take your time
this morning
(evening, afternoon)
chores and tasks
will wait.

There are hours enough
for you to
remember
who you are
before you begin
to move, to do
so that doing
will come
out of
being

Your whole being
your whole heart
your whole spirit
your whole you.

It Always Does

Peace to all you didn't get done today
because you were tired, couldn't focus
or really bring yourself to care.

Peace to the extra work later
the slow building of pressure

And peace to the day
when you rally and catch up.

It will come, it always does.

Meanwhile, darling

(((breathe)))

THAT PARTICULAR SKY

You can't always have views of the sunset
from your house.
For example, sometimes you live in a
duplex
where the western side is entirely blocked
by the other house
or sometimes there are bigger houses all
around you

Or, like now, where trees block the view in
the summer
and the porch is too cold to sit on when
the trees are bare
But if you stand in your pantry and lean
toward the fading light
you can see a corner of it

You can't always have views of the sunset
from your house,
but please don't think that you are doing
something wrong
with your life, your work, your love

Because even those with great jobs,
handsome lovers, and the best 401Ks
sometimes don't have views
of fiery reds and oranges
or every pastel in the palette
against the sharp outline of bare tree
branches
the gentle sorrow with the promise of
morning joy

Or, even if they do, they're not always wise
enough
to find the room where it happens
especially if it's the lowly pantry
and to lean the certain way you have to lean
in that particular house, toward that
particular sky
in that particular way that only you have
of seeing, and being seen.

Unannounced and Dancing

Depression feels like the same day over
and over
lying down in the dark, waking in the dark

Everything gray like mid-winter
like piles of dirty snow
and the clank of radiators.

But then March comes
and you start to notice the small differences
between one day and the next:

Today the sun set a bit later.
Today your hair needed a wash.
Today the birds were singing louder.

Today your back hurt less, but your
knees more.

And sometimes even the differences feel
so heavy
But then there are the moments when,
suddenly

Joy comes briefly
unannounced
and dancing.

This will not last forever.
Something will shift, I promise.

Not Quite That Poor

How many times do
friends have to say
they're glad to see me
and I look great

Before I stop wishing
I'd had time
to put on lipstick
on the way there?

And how long
will I count my pennies
when I buy
a cup of coffee

Before I realize
that in friends and in coins
I am no longer
quite that poor?

WARMTH AND SOFTNESS

If you are overwhelmed with decisions today
why not let your body make some of them?

She has been taking care of you for so long.

Listen to her fatigue, her hunger
not as things to overcome, but as wisdom.

If she is tired, rest.
If she is hungry, eat.

If her muscles are clenched as tightly as bones
stretch, gently stretch.

Let her warmth and softness
be your warmth and softness.

Rest safely in her arms.

COMPLICATIONS III

Science has proved that racism is a direct cause of physi-ological and psychological maladies...Further, experts have recently made connections to how chronic stress affects us at the cellular level and is passed down generationally.

~ Mary-Frances Winters, *Black Fatigue: How Racism Erodes the Mind, Body, and Spirit*

What I want to say here
is that I know words aren't going to fix things
and action is needed—my action—
to make this a safe country for your
body, mind, and spirit

But also that depression is hard enough
without all of this other pain as well.

And I see you.
And I believe you.
And it's not okay.
And your life, and health, matter.

THE GOSPEL OF THE SONGBIRDS

Today's forecast is "hazy, then rain"
and I hate to argue with the meteorologists

But despite the dull, gray sky
and despite the cold grayness in my heart
and the heavy dampness of my skin

    The birds have been shouting about the
    sun all morning

And their hearty evangelism
is beginning to convince me
that there will, in fact, be sunshine
today, or soon.

    "I think I believe," I whisper back to them,

    "Keep singing and I might believe."

Human Emotions

I am human, and nothing human is alien to me.

~ Terence

Good morning, humans.
What do you feel today?
Fear, joy, grief
longing, anger, love
frustration, happiness
exhaustion, bewilderment
anxiety, amusement
hope?

I feel it, too

There is nothing in you
however wild or strange
that is not in me, too

There is nothing weird in me
that part of you does not
recognize

We are somehow each entirely,
beautifully unique
And the same, the same, the same.

WHEN IT BEGINS
TO END

Maybe you won't even recognize it at first. A lack of something doesn't always register. Like on days I don't have a migraine it often takes me several hours to notice. Life just feels normal. Maybe it will be like that when the depression ends. You'll get up, have breakfast, brush your teeth. Then, halfway through the day realize that the toothbrush weighed a normal amount again, you didn't have to struggle to lift it. Maybe the depression will be just as bad except for a few minutes after your first cup of coffee, and then the next day a few minutes more. Maybe it will be more like dawn when you're camping, when there still is no discernable light in the sky but you notice you can see your own hands slightly better than before. Maybe you'll still have to wait what seems like forever for the light, and even longer for the sun itself. Maybe it will be more like spring, with false starts and snowfall over already-green grass, shivering because you turned your heat off too soon. I can't tell you how the depression will lift. But I can tell you that it is spring as I'm writing this and I used to think that winter would never end. I can tell you that the pain is not only better, it has been transformed into depth of understanding and empathy and determination. The leaves still sometimes shiver in the cool breeze, but they are green again. And I am hoping with you that the spring will be here soon for you, too.

BIRDSONG AND
BREATH

The birds are singing, the sun is shining
and we are all still carrying deep fear
or grief
or betrayal
or anger
or desperation.

There is room in this day for all of it.

Let the sun and birdsong
and your own brave breath
carry you through each painful moment
(breathe)
to the next joyful one (breathe here, too)

Until you find that you are living a
beautiful life
despite everything.

WARM BREEZE

As I prayed for my friends, a warm breeze—
one of the first warm breezes of spring—
came through the window

And it brought such joy and hope
that I turned it into my prayer.

Let their suffering end, I prayed
like the spring brings an end to the winter.

Let their skin transmit hope
as mine is doing right now
as it lost the ability to do
when the depression was bad.

I pray a warm breeze on your bare arms
a warm breeze triggering dopamine in
your mind
a warm breeze thawing your soul
bearing joy through the window
like a white dandelion seed, dancing.

DRUNKEN GATEKEEPERS

Someone got the gatekeepers drunk

they're laughing and swinging on their
gates

letting everyone in

Pass it on, tonight we all run through

God's garden, as much as we please

Tomorrow we'll brew beans we picked
there

into strong coffee, and offer it to

the sheepish, hungover guards.

FLESH AND STARDUST

Take deep and tender

care of yourself today.

Eat when you're hungry.

Let yourself feel what you feel.

Be your own best friend, your body's
advocate,

your spirit's protector.

Be stardust and soft, warm flesh.

Be a safe place for your own heart to live.

Something always shifts.

THE PLACE BETWEEN YOUR EYEBROWS

Peace to your knotted muscles
hunched shoulders
aching back, sore feet

Peace to the place
between your eyebrows
that cramps from frowning

Peace to the injury
that will not heal because
you can't afford to rest

Peace to your dear heart
that beats too hard
and too sad
sometimes.

DON'T BE AFRAID

What if curiosity

is the gateway drug

to beauty?

What if doubt is not a dead end

but a dark, brambly path

deeper into our faith?

What if we don't have

to be afraid?

What if the slippery slope

leads right into the open arms

of God?

A BLESSING FOR THE SPIRIT

Today I anoint with oil
your true, inner self.

I sprinkle holy water over
your connection to God,
to nature, and to your own
unique, sacred being.

I bless your brave, battered spirit
which still rises and falls
rises and falls.

I ordain your spirit
to be a sacred minister
of truth
and of grace.

Your Dear Heart

Throughout the world today
scary things are happening

Big, bright bells are rung
sirens sounding emergency, urgent

But within your house
and within your body

Is a heart battered but unbroken
fluttering, fighting to thrive

And I,

in my house

want to hear more

from that

dear

heart.

NOT A GRADED
EXERCISE

It's not that you're bad
at finding the right thing to say
to make it better
to keep the peace
to please everyone

It's that sometimes the right words
don't exist
And the wrong ones might wound
But saying nothing might, too.

It's not a graded exercise.
There is no way to get 100%.
It's just life, and love and—
if I may be so bold—

I will use my red marker
to give us both an A for effort
and permission to apologize without
self-hatred
and to try again without fear.

A Prayer for Springing Forward

May the new light mean new glimmers of
hope this year.
May each new minute of light mean new
health.
May we awake with a sliver more of
energy
and enter the evening with a handful more
of peace and grace.

May the wise, long nights still teach us
how to deepen
our faith, our love, and our empathy
and may the brave, lengthening days teach
us how to widen
our faith, our love, and our compassion.

THE WOMEN

The angels have been weeping
for much longer than we have.
Today's headlines do not catch
them by surprise. They have caught
women falling from fright
falling from the souring
of adrenaline after fighting off
the last person in the world
they thought they would have to fight.

The angels have been weeping
since the dawn of man
since men were given power
over women and children—or took it.
They have seen power corrupt
again and again, knowing full well
that only true communion heals.
Communion of the saints, not hierarchy.

The archangels know this particularly well
only grasping power when God insists
and letting go of it the first chance they get
(the handle of a flaming sword burns, too).

    The angels have been weeping, and
weep still
today, joined by us who wake to new
headlines.
They could tell us about the fall of legends
they know the epic tales, but know, too
the quiet trauma not often written
of the women these falling heroes fall against
burning them like kindling,
like a minor character, a side plot.

    But the angels know the powerless
are at the center of God's Eye
the center of the universe
though the headlines
speak only
of corruption
and of power.

A Short To-Do List
for the Day

Acknowledge that life is hard
and often painful

Notice that life is nevertheless
startlingly beautiful

Make art in some small way—
a poem, a line of prose, a drawing, a song

Love yourself the way you dream of
being loved

Take care of someone else in some
small way—
a call, a text, a prayer, a song

LONDON BRIDGE

(Content Warning: Suicide)

One of them, an expert in the law, tested him with this question: "Teacher, which is the greatest commandment in the Law?"
Jesus replied: "Love the Lord your God with all your heart and with all your soul and with all your mind." This is the first and greatest commandment. And the second is like it: "Love your neighbor as yourself."

~ Matthew 22:35–39 NIV

A few years ago in London a man climbed over the rail on a bridge with the intention to end his life. Passersby gathered around him and, reaching through the railing, held on to him for two hours to keep him safe until help arrived. The *Sun* posted a photo of the moment when the man was locked in an embrace with strangers. In the photo you can see the tension in the muscles of the passersby, the pain and struggle in their faces and the face of the man whose life they were saving. One man's arms are wrapped around his neck, their faces as close as lovers. Another squats near his feet, arms clutching his legs—we cannot see this man's face because he has chosen a position of discomfort and service over one of glory.

Whom do you identify with in the photo? The man whose desperation led him to climb over the railing of the bridge? See how he is held, how much even these strangers value his life. You are loved like that, whether you feel it right now or not. We need you. We can't do this without you. Stay.

Do you identify with the strangers? Can you feel the man's calves under your arms, shaking with the fear of death and the fear of hope? Are you afraid you cannot save the ones you love, much less your neighbor? See how the community works together, each taking their part, working together to hold safe the one who is in crisis. Even if you can only grasp one sinewy calf in your hand, you are needed. You are loved, and you are necessary. We can't do this without you. Come. Stay.

THAT ONE EVENING

There are years that ask questions and years that answer.

~ Zora Neale Hurston, *Their Eyes Were Watching God*

Peace to the years that ask questions
and the years that answer them.

Peace to the months that present
well-thought-out arguments
with charts and diagrams.

Peace to that one evening
that tears them all down.

Peace to the days asking energy
and nights answering rest.

Peace to your rest.

BE GENTLE

Be gentle with yourselves today. Both ancient wisdom and modern research show that allowing yourself to feel anger, grief, sorrow, jealousy, fear—all the so-called negative emotions—lets your brain process them and move on. The key is to not identify with them, not to grasp on to them or judge them. Acknowledge them, greet them, even, but, as Liz Gilbert puts it, don't let them drive the car. There are lots of ways to do this, but perhaps the simplest is just to say, to yourself or to a friend, "I feel sad today." It's not a problem that needs to be fixed. You're just a human being, living in a world that is sometimes sad. Or, "I feel angry," or scared, or jealous. You're a human being, living in a sometimes infuriating, frightening, and unfair world. Let yourself feel what you feel. And when you become a safe place for your feelings, joy, happiness, love, peace, and hope may visit more frequently, too.

BRAVE AND BELOVED

Peace to feelings
that overwhelm. Sorrow, frustration
disappointment, anger, fear.

Feelings that cannot find release
and lodge instead
in your stomach, head,
knotted muscles in your
back, shoulders, neck.

Peace, oh peace, to your
brave heart and your
beloved, tired body.

TEN THINGS I LIKE ABOUT YOU

Life is hard but you keep trying.

You have a unique way of looking at the world—I love seeing it through your eyes.

Speaking of eyes, yours are gorgeous.

When you laugh they kind of crinkle up at the corners.

When you laugh the world feels a little lighter.

You're carrying so much, but you still think of others.

You're unlearning old, harmful ways of doing things and finding better ones.

Your tears make me feel like it's okay
to cry.

Your tears tell the truth when you don't
have words.

You keep showing up. You're here. You're
still here.

Can you feel things starting to shift?

A Deeper Wisdom

There is a deeper wisdom inside of you
if you can sit with uncertainty for a while.

Let all your thoughts and feelings have
their say.
There's no need to choose one and write
your name on it.

Listen

    wait

till they

    quiet

down

    Then you will hear

(in your own voice)

    a gentle

suggestion.

How to Say "I Love You" to Someone Who Is Depressed II

"I don't understand what you're going through, but I want to. Can you tell me how you're feeling?"

"Call me anytime."

"I can't talk on the phone much but I will read every text, email, or message that you send me."

"I can't _____ but I can _____."

"I can't _____ but it is not because you are too needy; it's just that my resources are limited."

"Can I help you find someone to talk to?"

"Can I bring you a meal? Ice cream?"

"We are going to get through this together."

"You are not alone."

"I love you."

WE NEED YOU

The world needs you.

We need you.

We need you to take care of yourself
so you can offer the world
a healthy, true version of you
instead of an exhausted, guilt-ridden one

Listen to the birds, and the wind
and your own soft body

Don't jump into the fray too soon
but when you can, how you can
we need you.

UNFINISHED THINGS

Peace to the things you left undone
the book abandoned, scarf half-knit

The call you meant to make
the friendship never rekindled

The time you did your hair
and then stayed home

Peace to the things that made no
difference in the end
and those that may have.

Peace to the never knowing.

THE WIDER TABLE

Ah, Beloved, I see you
so hungry for love
that you starve yourself
beg for crumbs
at a table built only for a few.

Come to the wider table.

Come to the feast.

Come to the place where God and love
aren't a choice between, but the same.

Come and be what you have always
been—
loved, and loved, and loved.

LET US LOVE

Please let us be healthy, and if we can't
be healthy
let us take care of each other in our illness.

Let us be kind, and when we are not kind
let us be honest and apologize, and try again.

Let us be together, and when we can't be
together
let us feel that we are not alone in our
loneliness.

Let us be okay, and when we are not okay
when we are really nowhere near okay
let us acknowledge each other's suffering
and not be afraid of each other's pain

In other words
let us love, let us love, let us love.

HARD TIMES COME AGAIN NO MORE

'Tis the song, the sigh of the weary
Hard times, hard times, come again no more
Many days you have lingered around my cabin door
Oh, hard times, come again no more.

~ Stephen Foster

Hard times, let's have a chat

because I feel like you have maybe

worn out your welcome a little bit.

Not that the lessons you bring aren't
helpful
and I'm sure our character has been built a
lot by now—
So thanks for that.

But if we're honest, we would like the
chance
to see how easy living feels for a while
without constant crisis, constant struggle
just simple joy and happiness for a change.

But we won't forget you, hard times
how could we when our body keeps the
score?
We will write to you often, in our journals
and memoirs
but, oh, hard times, hard times
please come again no more.

LIVING IN THE AFTER

Oh, bless this strange new world.

We longed so long
for a returning
but found the path did not
wind back on itself
but forged ahead into the woods
into the brambles
and we're forced to forge with it.

And, oh! It all feels
So uncomfortable, uncertain, unfamiliar.

And yet, despite everything
a small green shoot of hope grows
within us
fresh and new as spring.

A BLESSING FOR DEPRESSION

May you feel better, and in the meantime
may you feel what you feel, without guilt
or shame or pressure.

May you recover your energy and hope,
and in the meantime
be accepted and cared for and carried.

May your suffering end, and not only end
may it be redeemed. And in the meantime

May you find a moment or two of
distraction in each day
and maybe even a moment of joy
and may those moments cling together

like droplets seeking each other on a
windowpane
till they become a full glass of water

And, Beloved,
may you drink
may you drink.

EPILOGUE

I'm starting to see a light

in the evening

at the end of the tunnel

in my own tired eyes

and in yours.

This will not last forever.

This did not last forever.

Acknowledgments

I wrote most of this book during a pandemic, with a knee injury, recovering from foot surgery, living alone, in a third-floor apartment with stairs I could barely navigate. Remarkably, none of this triggered another major depressive episode, which I can only attribute to the amazing people who held up ends of the net for me.

Thank you so much to Gina, Mark, Kate, Sarah, my mom, and my aunts Deb and Diane for being my phone-a-friend, text-a-friend, and email-a-friend lifelines.

Thank you to Judi for taking care of me post-surgery, Miriam for teaching me healing exercises and for setting a table for me and others, in person and over Zoom, and Ivy for practicing spiritual direction on me and being an amazing listener and co-explorer of our faith.

Thank you to my parents and brother for their love, support, and encouragement.

Thank you to Lisa for wanting to partner with me again and to Broadleaf for their creative collaboration on the concept of this book.

Thank you for the support from my writer friends, Matt, Kate, Laura, Judith, Tetyana, Glennon, Charlotte, Sarah, Bunmi, Danielle, Brad, Kaitlin, Amanda, Shannon, and so many others who are such a generous community to me.

And thank you to everyone who has read my first two books, or my online benedictions, and retweeted or shared or put them to music or read them to your congregation or sent them to your friends. It's because of you that I'm able to keep doing this work that I love.

NOTES

nothing human is alien to me: Frederick W. Ricord, *The Self-Tormentor (Heautontimorumenos) from the Latin of Publius Terentius Afer with More English Songs from Foreign Tongues* (New York: Charles Scribner, 1885), 25.

You expected to be sad: Ernest Hemingway, *A Moveable Feast* (New York: Scribner, 1964), 48.

You see, one loves: Antoine de Saint Exupéry, *The Little Prince* (Orlando, FL: Harcourt Brace & Company, 1943), 26.

a great battle: Often attributed to Plato or Philo of Alexandria, but probably originally penned by Ian Maclaren in the 1897 Christmas edition of the *British Weekly*. Source: https://en.wikipedia.org/wiki/Ian_Maclaren.

Conditions described as comorbidities: Sherry Christiansen, "What is Comorbidity?" *Verywell Health*, February 4, 2021, accessed May 31, 2021, https://www.verywellhealth.com/comorbidity-5081615.

to let sadnesses visit: Jonny Sun, *Goodbye, Again: Essays, Reflections, and Illustrations* (New York: Harper Perennial, 2021), 196.

an invincible summer: Albert Camus, *Return to Tipasa*, Genius, accessed June 19, 2021, https://genius.com/Albert-camus-return-to-tipasa-annotated.

Hopelessly lost and nearly found: Laura Parrott Perry, used with permission.

These divine sparks: Rabbi Amy Eilberg, "Sparks of Holiness Hidden Deep within the Darkness," The Jewish News of Northern California, June 20, 2003, accessed May 2, 2021, https://www.jweekly.com/2003/06/20/sparks-of-holiness-hidden-deep-within-the-darkness/.

Come for a walk with me: Jessica Kantrowitz, *The Long Night: Readings and Stories to Help You through Depression* (Minneapolis, MN: Fortress Press, 2020), 1–2.

the yearning soul is the nightingale: Sister Wendy Beckett, "The Intoxicating Eye: On Looking at Jila Peacock's Ten Poems from Hafez," *Image Journal* no. 51: https://imagejournal.org/article/the-intoxicating-eye/.

You are my beloved: Henri Nouwen with Philip Roderick, *Beloved: Henri Nouwen in Conversation* (Grand Rapids, MI: William B. Eerdmans, 2007), 38.

in a very foreign tongue: Rainer Maria Rilke, *Letters to a Young Poet,* trans. M. D. Herter Norton (New York: Norton & Company, 1934), 35.

now forever lost: Andrew Solomon, *The Noonday Demon: An Atlas of Depression* (New York: Scribner, 2001), 208.

Grief is depression in proportion: Andrew Solomon, *The Noonday Demon* (New York: Scribner, 2001), 16.

What is grief but love persevering: *WandaVision,* season 1, episode 8, "Previously On," written by Laura Donney, directed by Matt Shakman, aired February 26, 2021, on Disney+.

he realized that the frost was over: C. S. Lewis, *The Lion, The Witch, and The Wardrobe* (New York: HarperCollins, 1950), 128–129.

NOTES

A great Shadow has departed: J. R. R. Tolkien, *The Return of the King* (New York: Ballantine Books, 1965), 283.

racism is a direct cause: Mary-Frances Winters, *Black Fatigue: How Racism Erodes the Mind, Body, and Spirit* (Oakland, CA: Berrett-Koehler, 2020), 4–5.

a photo of the moment: Nigel Howard, photograph, accessed May 11, 2021, https://www.thesun.co.uk/news/3442253/man-restrained-by-crowds-for-two-hours-after-threatening-to-jump-from-bridge-in-north-london/.

There are years that ask questions: Zora Neale Hurston, *Their Eyes Were Watching God* (New York: HarperCollins, 2006), 21.

hard times, come again no more: Stephen Foster, *Hard Times Come Again No More* (New York: Firth, Pond & Co.), 1854.